Uncovering American History™

A Primary Source Investigation of The Gold Rush

Melanie Gildenstein and
Kerri O'Donnell

rosen publishing's rosen central®

Published in 2016 by The Rosen Publishing Group, Inc.
29 East 21st Street, New York, NY 10010

First Edition

Library of Congress Cataloging-in-Publication Data

Gildenstein, Melanie.
A primary source investigation of the gold rush/Melanie Gildenstein and Kerri O'Donnell.—First edition.
pages cm.—(Uncovering American history)
Includes bibliographical references and index.
ISBN 978-1-4994-3511-5 (library bound)
1. California—Gold discoveries—Juvenile literature. 2. California—Gold discoveries—Sources—Juvenile literature. I. O'Donnell, Kerri, 1972- II. Title.
F865.G45 2015
979.4'04–dc23

2015000016

Manufactured in the United States of America

CONTENTS

INTRODUCTION

Gold. Timelessly precious. Always in demand. Try to imagine living in America in the 1840s, say, 1848, the year that the now-famous gold rush in America began. There's no such thing as public schooling yet, so chances are that you live and work on a farm. Or in your parents' store, living above it. The Civil War won't be fought for another ten years, so if you're a black American, depending on where you live, you may still be enslaved. Statistically, most Americans at this point live in the eastern half of the country. There are thirty states; California isn't one of them—it just became a U.S. territory in the beginning of the year, thanks to the U.S. victory in the Mexican War. The only means of communication is word of mouth and newspapers. Travel is done on foot, by horse, or by boat. (The first transcontinental train to California won't run until 1869.)

Being the smart, self-taught young person that you are, you read *The New York Herald* of August 29, 1848, and learn that there's a gold rush going on way out west

This 1902 illustration shows travelers taking a route known as the Overland Trail—a route that they and so many others in the mid-1800s hoped would lead them to gold.

at a place called Sutter's Mill in California. (Actually, the gold rush had been going on for a while, but news traveled slowly back then.) So what would you do? Would you want to make the journey and see if you could strike it rich?

Hundreds of thousands of people did just that—people from all over the world, in fact. Between 1848 and the mid-1850s, California's population nearly tripled—to just shy of half a million people. You know now why they went. But did most people get what they came for? Did they strike it rich? Read on and find out.

CHAPTER ONE

A FLASH OF LIGHT IN THE DITCH

Two gold nuggets. Just sitting there in a ditch. It was January 24, 1848, in Coloma, California—not too far from the point in eastern California where the border heading straight southward takes a turn to the east. A handyman named James Wilson Marshall made a discovery in a California river that would change the course of American history. On that winter morning, Marshall was going about his business, working for his employer, Johann Augustus Sutter. Sutter had assigned Marshall the task of overseeing construction of a sawmill. What Marshall found in the river near the mill that day would change both men's lives—and indeed that of the entire country—forever. Marshall had found gold.

"I HAVE FOUND IT"

The drawing on page 8 was done by Marshall's own hand and illustrates what is widely considered to be the most important event in California's history—Marshall's discovery of gold at Sutter's Mill. Although

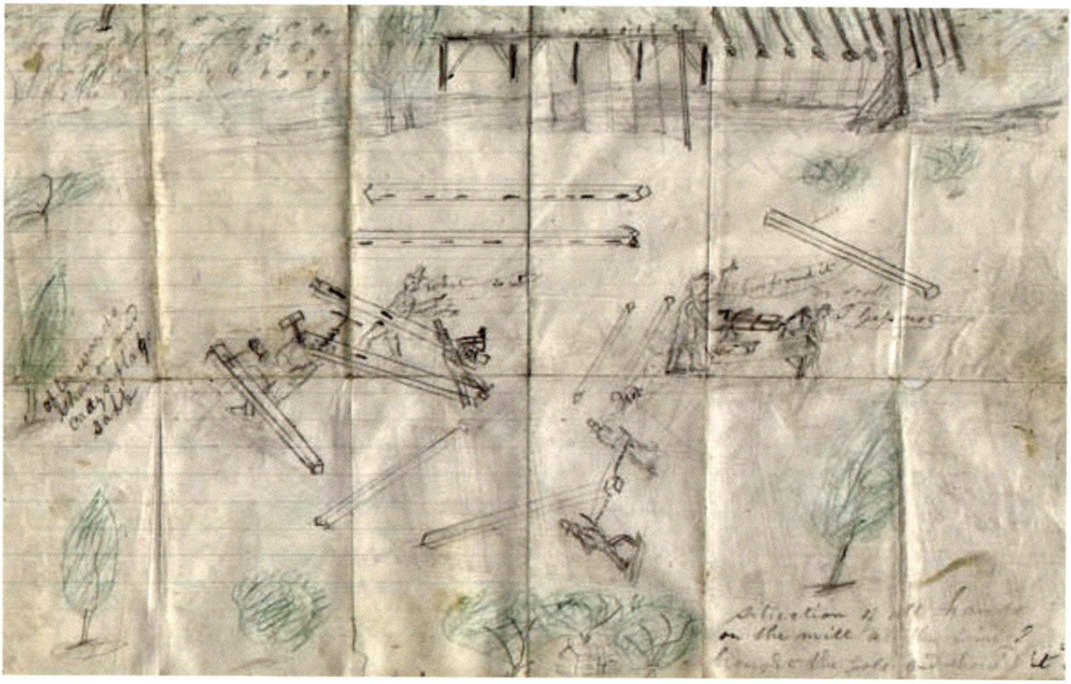

This sketch was found in James Marshall's cabin near Placerville, California. A man named John Sipp bought the property after Marshall's death in 1885. In 1910 Sipp gave the drawing to the California State Library.

the exact date of the sketch is unknown, it is clear that Marshall drew it soon after finding the gold. On the lower right-hand side, Marshall wrote, "Situation of all hands on the mill at the time I brought the gold and show'd it." A mill worker on the left-hand side of the drawing says, "What is it?" Marshall, at the right, responds, "I have found it." A carpenter named William Scott, to the right of Marshall, says, "I guess not." According to historians, it is likely that the sketch re-creates the dialogue that took place at the mill immediately following Marshall's discovery.

SUTTER'S FORT

The gold in that California river might have gone undiscovered if Marshall had not come to work for Johann Sutter—or John Sutter, as he came to be known. Sutter was a Swiss businessman who came to America to make his fortune. After pursuing many unsuccessful business ventures, Sutter settled in California in 1839. At that time, California was still part of Mexico. Sutter persuaded California's governor, Juan Bautista Alvarado, to give him a land grant of nearly 50,000 acres (20,234 ha) in California's northern Central Valley. There, on a piece of the land where the Sacramento and American Rivers meet, he built what came to be known as Sutter's Fort.

Sutter's Fort became the headquarters for his business ventures. He tried his hand at farming and raising livestock, hoping to strike it rich by supplying the public with flour, beef, and leather. He needed people to work for him, so he employed groups of Native American laborers from the area, such as the Yalisumni Nisenan Indians. Sutter paid them with items they needed, such as blankets, clothing, and tools. When he couldn't find enough manpower, he sometimes rounded up Native Americans by force and made them work at gunpoint. Sutter also needed workers with the skills necessary to make his new "colony" self-sufficient. He needed men who could build new workshops so that he could produce more products to grow his empire. His plan was to build a town near Sutter's Fort, a place where emigrating settlers from the east could build their homes and thus spend their money on his products. The problem of finding enough workers was solved as more people began to emigrate west during the 1840s.

MARSHALL AND THE SAWMILL

James Marshall was one such emigrant, an experienced craftsman born in New Jersey in 1810 who could carry out complex jobs. A new town would need lumber, and Sutter wanted to establish himself as the leading lumber supplier in the region. Marshall began working for Sutter, overseeing the building of a sawmill to process the lumber. In August 1847, Marshall found the ideal spot for Sutter's Mill—the small town of Coloma. Coloma was on the southern part of the American River, about forty miles (sixty-four kilometers) east of Sutter's Fort.

WHAT HE SAW AT THE MILL

The sawmill was finished in January 1848. Marshall's men had begun deepening the stream near the mill to allow more water to flow to the mill wheel, which would increase the waterpower the mill needed to operate. On the morning of January 24, 1848, Marshall went down to the river to see how work was progressing. As he stood there, he saw a shining flash of light in the ditch and reached down to see what was there. It was gold.

ONE FOR THE BOOKS... AND THE NEWSPAPERS

Because Marshall was such an important part of California's history, many books were written about his life. One, called *The Life and Adventures of James W. Marshall, The Discoverer of Gold in California*, was written by George Frederick Parsons and is considered one of the most important historical books about California. Shown below is the title page from the book. The illustration depicts Marshall holding a nugget of gold in his hand.

After Marshall made the discovery, he quickly went to Sutter's Fort to tell Sutter the news. Sutter didn't believe Marshall at first but quickly changed his mind when Marshall put the gold on a nearby table. Marshall led Sutter to the sawmill and Sutter inspected the site himself, using his knife to extract another lump of gold from a nearby gorge.

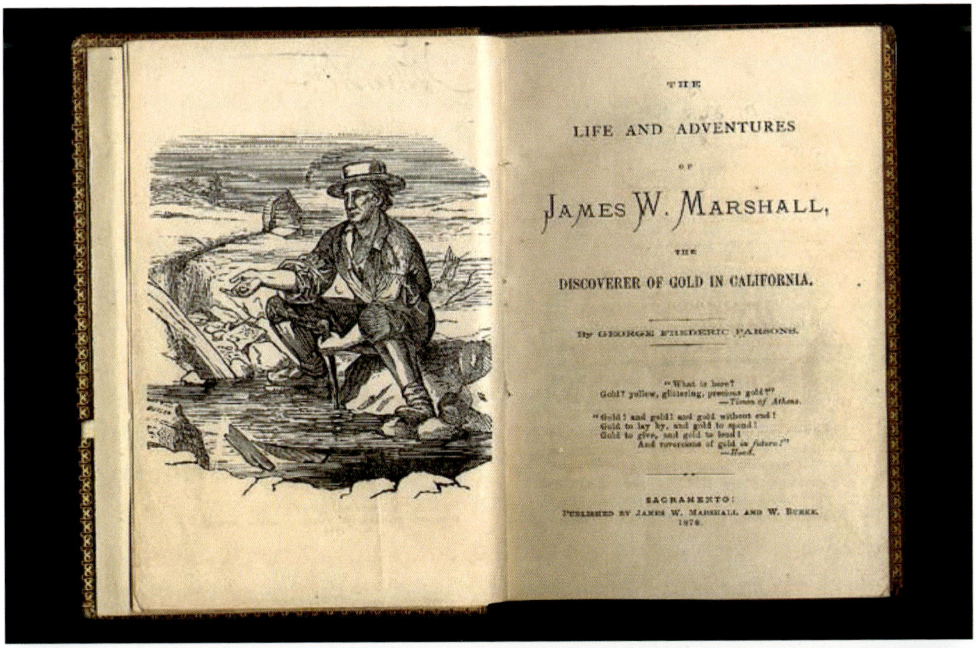

THE

LIFE AND ADVENTURES

OF

JAMES W. MARSHALL,

THE

DISCOVERER OF GOLD IN CALIFORNIA.

By GEORGE FREDERIC PARSONS.

"What is here?
Gold? yellow, glittering, precious gold?"
—*Timon of Athens.*

"Gold! and gold! and gold without end!
Gold to lay by, and gold to spend!
Gold to give, and gold to lend!
And reversions of gold in *futuro!*"
—*Hood.*

SACRAMENTO:
PUBLISHED BY JAMES W. MARSHALL AND W. BURKE.
1870.

George Frederick Parsons's book about James Marshall was published in 1870. In it, Parsons recounts both Marshall's discovery of gold as well as his life of hard luck. Marshall hoped that the book would turn around his downward financial spiral, but it wasn't to be: in 1885 he died a poor man.

John Sutter's writings regarding his fateful meeting with Marshall and of their trip to the site the following day was printed in the *San Francisco Pacific News* on October 9, 1849. Although Marshall and Sutter intended to keep the discovery secret, this proved impossible. Sutter writes: "Notwithstanding our precautions not to be observed, as soon as we came back to the mill, we noticed the excitement of the working people . . . and to complete our disappointment, one of the Indians who had worked at the gold mine . . . cried out in showing to us some specimens which he picked up by himself—Oro!-Oro-Oro!!!"

Those Native American workers had also found *oro*—gold—and the news would soon spread throughout the land.

A WELL-TIMED LEASE

As it happens, just a few weeks before Marshall had found the gold, Sutter and Marshall tried to establish control of Coloma and the surrounding valley for their business plans. On January 1, 1848, just twenty-three days before Marshall found gold on the land, a lease was drafted so that Sutter's and Marshall's work could proceed without interruption. With Marshall's discovery of gold, control of the land became even more important. Sutter knew he had to control the Coloma Valley to keep his hands on the gold. He also knew that if a swarm of hopeful gold miners arrived, construction of his sawmill and a proposed gristmill would be delayed. He asked the construction crew to keep Marshall's discovery quiet, promising that they would be given time off to search for their own gold.

John Sutter's account of the events following Marshall's discovery were made into a "letter sheet"—stationery that could be personalized with a message, which was then folded and sealed to form its own envelope for mailing. This lithographed letter sheet was published in 1854 by San Francisco–based publishers Britton & Rey. The publishing company wanted to make money from Marshall's and Sutter's fame, hoping that emigrants who had come west would use the stationery to write to their loved ones in the East.

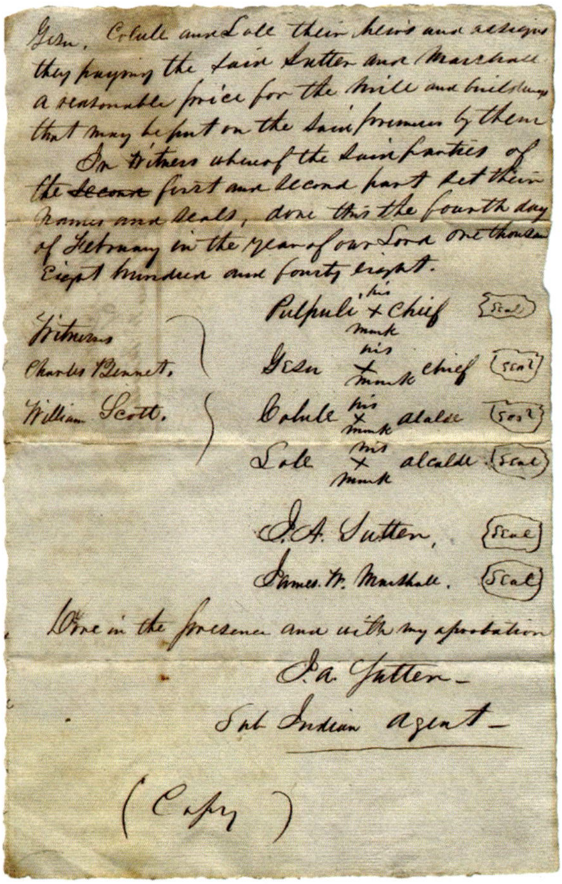

Gesu, Colule and Lole their heirs and assigns
they paying the said Sutter and Marshall
a reasonable price for the mill and buildings
that may be put on the said premises by them
In witness whereof the said parties of
the ~~second~~ first and second part set their
names and seals, done this the fourth day
of February in the year of our Lord one thousand
Eight hundred and forty eight.

Pulpuli his x mark Chief {Seal}

Witness
Charles Bennett,
William Scott.

Gesu his x mark chief (Seal)
Colule his x mark alcalde (Seal)
Lole his x mark alcalde (Seal)

J.A. Sutter, (Seal)
James W. Marshall. (Seal)

Done in the presence and with my approbation
J.A. Sutter
Sub Indian agent

(Copy)

Along with John Sutter's and James Marshall's signatures, the lease was also signed by two chiefs and two alcaldes from the Yalisumni tribe. (An alcalde was a head administrative and judicial officer of a Spanish town.) It is believed that the original lease was destroyed in a fire. This copy remains in the California State Library. (For a transcription and contemporary English translation, see page 51.)

REQUEST DENIED

Sutter and Marshall met with leaders of the Yalisumni Nisenan tribe to negotiate a lease for use of their tribal land in the Coloma Valley. The lease had originally been drafted on that same day—January 1, 1848—but it was not signed until February 4, 1848—eleven days after Marshall had discovered the gold and just two days after the United States had defeated Mexico in the Mexican War. That win took California away from Mexico and brought it under the control of the United States. Sutter wanted the approval of the military governor of California, Colonel Richard Barnes Mason. He sent Mason the lease, but Mason quickly rejected it, stating in a letter to Sutter, "The United States do not recognize the right of Indians to sell or lease lands on which they reside."

★ CHAPTER TWO

CALIFORNIA, HERE WE COME!

In 1848—from the winter through the spring—word of Marshall's discovery started trickling throughout California. At the mill itself, men working for Sutter left their jobs to search for gold, digging along the American River and its tributaries. In May of that year, news of the discovery of gold reached San Francisco, along with a sample of gold dust that was promptly displayed in public.

"Gold fever" hit hard, and large numbers of prospectors began traveling to the area. These gold seekers were called Argonauts, a reference to a tale in Greek mythology. In that story, a man named Jason went on a quest for the Golden Fleece, a fleece made of gold that a king had placed in a grove guarded by a fierce dragon. Jason's crew, the Argonauts (named for the ship they sailed in, the *Argo*), assisted him with his voyage. In 1848, a quest had begun—not for the Golden Fleece of Greek mythology, but for the gold of California. As the San Francisco paper the *Californian* noted in its May 29, 1848, edition: "The whole country, from San Francisco to Los Angeles, and from the sea shore to the base of the Sierra Nevadas, resounds with the sordid cry, '*gold*, GOLD, GOLD!' while the field is left half planted, the house half built, and everything neglected but the manufacture of shovels and pickaxes."

GOOD NEWS TRAVELS FAST—WELL, FAST FOR THE 1800s

News of the gold soon spread throughout the United States, across the Atlantic Ocean to Europe via ships, south into Mexico and South America, and west across the Pacific Ocean via trading vessels bound for Hawaii, China, and Australia. Marshall's discovery would lead to a massive migration. At first, most of the gold seekers who arrived in California were not from the United States. In 1848, there were no transcontinental telegraph lines or railroads that would allow for news to spread quickly across the country, and the trip on foot was slow and painful. Most news spread via ocean-going vessels—but this water-borne process was also a slow one.

Nonetheless, news of the gold strike in California traveled by ship south along the Pacific coast to the tip of South America and around Cape Horn, then up the Atlantic Coast to the eastern port cities of the United States. The trip could take up to seven months. Another route for spreading the news was taken by traveling down the Pacific coast by ship as far as the Isthmus of Panama—a thin piece of land that separated the Pacific Ocean from the Gulf of Mexico. Passengers then went on foot across the isthmus, and another boat would take them through the Caribbean to the East Coast. Though shorter than the Cape Horn route, this approach also took many weeks.

A ship traveling to China or South America could complete a trip in less time. For this reason, immigrants from other countries began to arrive in large numbers before people from the eastern United States even knew of the gold strike. When people in the eastern United States finally did hear the news, they often didn't believe the stories and stayed put. In June 1848, California's military governor, Richard Barnes Mason, set out to examine the gold district to see if all of the stories coming out of Coloma Valley were true. He toured the land around the American River and prepared a report on the great quantities of gold found in the region and sent it to Washington, D.C., along with a chest filled with gold.

Although *the New York Herald* of August 29, 1848, had reported news of the gold strike, it wasn't until December 5, 1848, when President James Polk acknowledged the validity of the strike to Congress that most people "back east" took notice. Within days of Polk's validation, the people of the eastern United States became overwhelmed by "gold fever." For many, the only cure was to head west to seek their fortune. Many who made the journey later returned east to give lectures on the topic, which stirred up even more interest in California. The mass migration was underway.

EXTRA, EXTRA: READ ALL ABOUT IT!

Different publications further helped spread the stories of California's golden treasure. Some of these publications took the form of broadsheets—large sheets of paper printed on one or both sides that could be reproduced in large quantities. These were handed out to the public or posted in public places, usually to generate interest in a lecture or presentation by someone who had been to California's gold mines. People might be charged a small sum to attend, and both the lecturer and the event's organizer could make a nice profit.

Books about California's gold were quickly written. One such book was written by a man named J. Ely Sherwood, who had traveled to California and decided to share his experiences with the gold-hungry public. His book—written in 1849 and published in New York—was entitled *The Pocket Guide to California; A Sea and Land Route Book, Containing a Description of the El Dorado . . . To Which Is Added the Gold-Hunter's Memorandum and Pocket Directory*. The book's long title mirrors the extensive information contained within—a discussion of the various routes to California by land and by sea, a description of California's geographical features, and

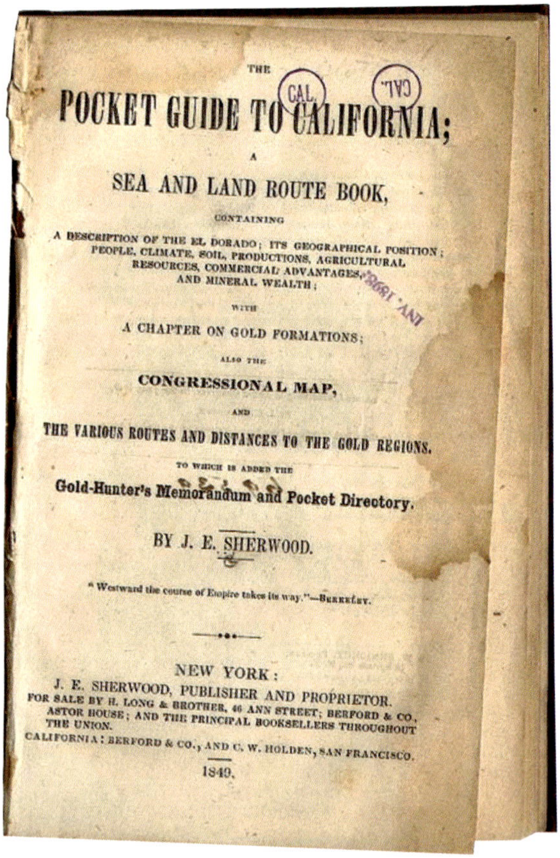
THE
POCKET GUIDE TO CALIFORNIA;
A
SEA AND LAND ROUTE BOOK,
CONTAINING
A DESCRIPTION OF THE EL DORADO; ITS GEOGRAPHICAL POSITION; PEOPLE, CLIMATE, SOIL, PRODUCTIONS, AGRICULTURAL RESOURCES, COMMERCIAL ADVANTAGES, AND MINERAL WEALTH;
WITH
A CHAPTER ON GOLD FORMATIONS;
ALSO THE
CONGRESSIONAL MAP,
AND
THE VARIOUS ROUTES AND DISTANCES TO THE GOLD REGIONS.
TO WHICH IS ADDED THE
Gold-Hunter's Memorandum and Pocket Directory.
BY J. E. SHERWOOD.
"Westward the course of Empire takes its way."—BERKELEY.
NEW YORK:
J. E. SHERWOOD, PUBLISHER AND PROPRIETOR.
FOR SALE BY H. LONG & BROTHER, 46 ANN STREET; BERFORD & CO., ASTOR HOUSE; AND THE PRINCIPAL BOOKSELLERS THROUGHOUT THE UNION.
CALIFORNIA: BERFORD & CO., AND C. W. HOLDEN, SAN FRANCISCO.
1849.

Many books published during the gold rush used sensationalism to sell copies. J. Ely Sherwood's book was no exception. Along with facts about California, Sherwood included advertisements for all kinds of strange merchandise for the hopeful miner.

a summation of California's "people, climate, soil, productions, agricultural resources, commercial advantages, and mineral wealth."

Only a few months had passed since James Marshall discovered gold, but hopeful gold seekers had all manner of written material on the subject at their fingertips. Books were published within months. Newspapers around the country jumped at the chance to use "gold fever" to sell papers in the winter of 1848 to 1849. The newspapers published story after story about the adventures of life out west, using every detail they could to fill their papers and meet their deadlines.

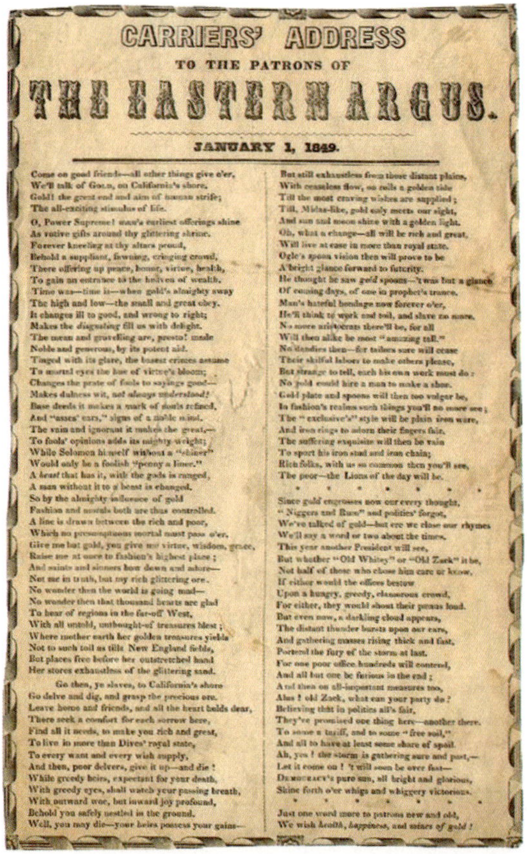

CARRIERS' ADDRESS

TO THE PATRONS OF

THE EASTERN ARGUS.

JANUARY 1, 1849.

Come on good friends—all other things give o'er,
We'll talk of GOLD, on California's shore,
Gold! the great end and aim of human strife;
The all-exciting stimulus of life.
O, Power Supreme! man's earliest offerings shine
As votive gifts around thy glittering shrine.
Forever kneeling at thy altars proud,
Behold a suppliant, fawning, cringing crowd,
There offering up peace, honor, virtue, health,
To gain an entrance to the heaven of wealth.
Time was—time is—when gold's almighty sway
The high and low—the small and great obey.
It changes ill to good, and wrong to right;
Makes the *disgusting* fill us with delight.
The mean and grovelling are, presto! made
Noble and generous, by its potent aid.
Tinged with its glare, the basest crimes assume
To mortal eyes the hue of virtue's bloom;
Changes the prate of fools to sayings good—
Makes dulness wit, *not always understood!*
Base deeds it makes a mark of souls refined,
And "asses' ears," signs of a noble mind.
The vain and ignorant it makes the great,—
To fools' opinions adds its mighty weight;
While Solomon himself without a "shiner"
Would only be a foolish "penny a liner."
A *beast* that has it, with the gods is ranged,
A man without it to a beast is changed.
So by the almighty influence of gold
Fashion and morals both are thus controlled.
A line is drawn between the rich and poor,
Which no presumptuous mortal must pass o'er.
Give me but gold, you give me virtue, wisdom, grace,
Raise me at once to fashion's highest place;
And saints and sinners bow down and adore—
Not me in truth, but my rich glittering ore.
No wonder then the world is going mad—
No wonder then that thousand hearts are glad
To hear of regions in the far-off West,
With all untold, unthought-of treasures blest;
Where mother earth her golden treasures yields
Not to such toil as tills New England fields,
But places free before her outstretched hand
Her stores exhaustless of the glittering sand.
Go then, ye slaves, to California's shore
Go delve and dig, and grasp the precious ore.
Leave home and friends, and all the heart holds dear,
There seek a comfort for each sorrow here,
Find all it needs, to make you rich and great,
To live in more than Dives' royal state,
To every want and every wish supply,
And then, poor delvers, give it up—and die!
While greedy heirs, expectant for your death,
With greedy eyes, shall watch your passing breath,
With outward woe, but inward joy profound,
Behold you safely nestled in the ground.
Well, you may die—your heirs possess your gains—
But still exhaustless from those distant plains,
With ceaseless flow, so rolls a golden tide
Till the most craving wishes are supplied;
Till, Midas-like, gold only meets our sight,
And sun and moon shine with a golden light.
Oh, what a change—all will be rich and great,
Will live at ease in more than royal state.
Ogle's spoon vision then will prove to be
A bright glance forward to futurity.
He thought he saw *gold* spoons—'twas but a glance
Of coming days, of one in prophet's trance.
Man's hateful bondage now forever o'er,
He'll think to work and toil, and slave no more.
No more aristocrats there'll be, for all
Will then alike be most "amazing tall."
No dandies then—for tailors sure will cease
Their skilful labors to make others please,
But strange to tell, each his own work must do:
No gold could hire a man to make a shoe.
Gold plate and spoons will then too vulgar be,
In fashion's realms such things you'll no more see;
The "exclusive's" style will be plain iron ware,
And iron rings to adorn their fingers fair.
The suffering exquisite will then be vain
To sport his iron stud and iron chain;
Rich folks, with us so common then you'll see,
The poor—the Lions of the day will be.
* * * * * * *
Since *gold* engrosses now our every thought,
"Niggers and Rum" and politics' forgot,
We've talked of gold—but ere we close our rhymes
We'll say a word or two about the times.
This year another President will see,
But whether "Old Whitey" or "Old Zack" it be,
Not half of those who chose him care or know,
If either would the offices bestow
Upon a hungry, greedy, clamorous crowd,
For either, they would shout their peans loud.
But even now, a darkling cloud appears,
The distant thunder bursts upon our ears,
And gathering masses rising thick and fast,
Portend the fury of the storm at last.
For one poor office hundreds will contend,
And all but one be furious in the end;
And then on all-important measures too,
Alas! old Zack, what can your party do?
Believing that in politics all's fair,
They've promised one thing here—another there.
To some a tariff, and to some "free soil,"
And all to have at least some share of spoil.
Ah, yes! the storm is gathering sure and past,—
Let it come on! 't will soon be over fast—
DEMOCRACY's pure sun, all bright and glorious,
Shine forth o'er whigs and whiggery victorious.
* * * * * * *
Just one word more to patrons new and old,
We wish *health*, *happiness*, and *stores of gold!*

A biblical reference in "Carriers' Address" warns of eternal damnation for people who seek only riches. (For a transcription, see page 52.)

There were countless firsthand accounts of ship passengers and captains who had made the trek west, detailing the journey and the strange new land that met them upon arrival. There were stories from the goldfields by those already hard at work digging for riches, and there were also incredible tales of wealth beyond one's wildest dreams. The newspapers published every official text available on the subject in order to convince people that the sometimes-outrageous stories they were printing on their pages were true. All these things fueled the fire already burning in would-be Argonauts' bellies and hastened their preparations for the journey west.

CURRIER AND IVES

In this 1849 lithograph by Nathaniel Currier, the subtitle reads, "An accurate drawing of the famous hill of gold, which has been put into a scow by the owner, and attached to a Sperm Whale who is now engaged in towing it around the Horn for New York." The man in the cartoon sits high atop a mound of gold that has been placed in a scow, a kind of flat-bottomed boat used mainly to haul large quantities of raw

This lithograph, entitled *California Gold*, is attributed to Nathan Currier, a partner in the famous New York City art firm Currier and Ives.

GOLD FEVER: A CAUSE FOR HUMOR OR CONCERN?

The newspapers were also full of endless editorial commentary poking fun at the new national obsession with California's gold. On January 1, 1849, the following poem appeared in an eastern newspaper called the *Eastern Argus.* It takes a satirical look at the gold fever that gripped the eastern United States during this time, as can be seen in these lines:

materials or garbage. The man–shown in typical upper-class attire, complete with top hat and umbrella–represents a stereotypical greedy "Yankee" from New York, intent on lugging home the vast riches he has accumulated in "El Dorado," the golden land of California.

THE DYNAMIC DUO

Nathaniel Currier, who in 1852 teamed up with James Merritt Ives, was responsible for this and other illuminating visual records we have of the gold rush–in fact of nineteenth-century America itself. While their methods and media were rendered obsolete by photography, the detail and craft went beyond that of political cartoons and photography both by use of inserted dialogue, offering us a feel for the mood and the manner of the day. The firm enjoyed great fame in the mid to late 1800s, producing more than 7,000 works about American life.

Come on good friends—all other things give o'er,
We'll talk of Gold, on California's shore,
Gold! The great end and aim of human strife;
The all-exciting stimulus of life . . .
Go then, ye slaves, to California's shore
Go delve and dig, and grasp the precious ore.

The writer expressed the opinion that the nation's obsession with riches had made people forget the truly important things in life. People were now "slaves" to gold and had given up everything that was truly good in life to find it.

Satirical views of the gold rush found their way into every aspect of American life. Artists used humorous drawings to convey their opinions about how the obsession with California's gold was affecting the politics, economy, and spirit of the United States. Many saw gold fever as a disease infecting the morality of the entire nation, a growing greed that was making people neglect their ideals and values in order to make a quick fortune.

★ CHAPTER THREE

GOLD SEEKERS SET SAIL

Gold fever was something unto itself. No medication could loosen its grip. So once gold fever hit the East, there was no stopping it. People headed to California in huge numbers. (That is, men headed to California in huge numbers; the gold rush was a male-dominated event. According to the History Channel, by 1852, more than 90 percent of the people prospecting for gold were men.)

After President Polk's address to Congress in late 1848, an estimated 1,400 vessels soon set sail for California from the United States and Canada alone. Easterners from the seafaring cities and towns of New England and the Mid-Atlantic states usually made the journey by ship, heading out from the nearest port. They were often called forty-niners, a reference to the year 1849, when they left their homes in search of gold.

As more easterners headed west, the results of the mass migration to California were felt strongly in smaller eastern communities where the population was noticeably reduced. The island of Nantucket, off the coast of Massachusetts, was one such community. During the late 1700s,

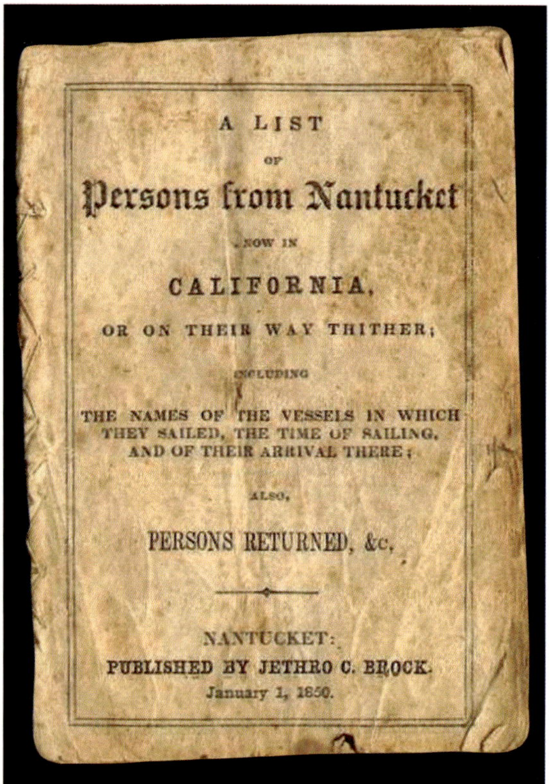
A LIST
OF
Persons from Nantucket
NOW IN
CALIFORNIA,
OR ON THEIR WAY THITHER;
INCLUDING
THE NAMES OF THE VESSELS IN WHICH THEY SAILED, THE TIME OF SAILING, AND OF THEIR ARRIVAL THERE;
ALSO,
PERSONS RETURNED, &c.

NANTUCKET:
PUBLISHED BY JETHRO C. BROCK.
January 1, 1850.

The cover of a twenty-four page book published on January 1, 1850, by a man named Jethro C. Brock of Nantucket, Massachusetts. It provides a listing of 650 people from the island who had gone to California or were en route there at the beginning of 1850.

Nantucket had become one of the world's largest whaling centers. By 1850, though, whaling was in decline, and many people from the area set out to find gold instead.

WATER, WATER EVERYWHERE

Some easterners sailed south, down the eastern coast, around Cape Horn at the southernmost tip of South America and then up the Pacific coast, finally reaching San Francisco Bay. It is estimated that as many as sixteen thousand people traveled to California via the Cape Horn route in 1849, followed by about twelve thousand more people in 1850. Those who wanted a quicker voyage chose a route that combined both sea and land travel. They sailed to the Isthmus of Panama, where they would cross the narrow strip of land on foot and board a northbound ship for the trip up the Pacific coast to California.

On page 25 is a typical map of the period. It shows the main water routes that were traveled to reach California from

This 1849 map of the water routes to California was originally in a travel book of that year by T. J. Farnham about his travels. The map was probably printed in larger quantities after the book was published: people were hungry for any information about the journey west for gold.

the East—either around Cape Horn or through the Isthmus of Panama, also known as Chagres. The western part of the United States is shown on the left, and Central and South America appear on the right. The yellow-shaded area shows the region where gold was found. Included on the map are two text boxes. The text box on the left is entitled "Important Directions to Persons Emigrating to California." The box on the right is entitled "Description of California, or the New Gold Region" and contains the following words, "Such is California—the richest, most picturesque and beautiful region, for its extent, upon the face of the earth."

LIFE AT SEA

The seemingly endless days aboard ships bound for California were filled with other dangers, too. Many passengers got scurvy, a disease caused by lack of vitamin C. It was difficult to keep up a supply of vitamin C–rich fruits and vegetables on the ship—these foods quickly went bad. Scurvy causes bleeding gums, loose teeth, and swollen, blackened legs. Chills and delirium often set in, and death sometimes follows.

Whether coming up along the Pacific coast from Cape Horn or from Panama, many ships had to sail out to the Sandwich Islands (now called Hawaii) before they could even catch the winds they needed to take them to the port of San Francisco. Boredom became an issue—after spending so much time at sea, passengers desperately needed some kind of entertainment. They became quite creative in finding ways to amuse themselves, putting out ship newspapers or staging plays to pass the time. Although the promise of gold was all most people needed to embark on a voyage west, some ship owners made up persuasive advertisements that listed all the comforts of their ships, hoping to fill their cabins with customers who would pay well for safe passage to California.

DANGEROUS WATERS

The trip around Cape Horn by boat took about six months and brought passengers through hazardous waters. Upon reaching the waters around "the Horn," a ship would lurch due to the turbulent currents, and huge waves would crash over the deck. The winds were freezing, and sometimes ships were blown farther south toward Antarctica. It usually took about a month to complete this part of the trip around the Horn. The voyage was usually made by young, strong men who were seeking adventure.

The route via the Isthmus of Panama (or Chagres) was shorter and could be made in two months if there were no major delays, but it was also a difficult trip. Once ships from the East reached Panama, passengers had to travel about 75 miles (120 km) up the Chagres River to cross the isthmus, then travel another 25 miles (40 km) by mule through the jungle to get to Panama City. At Panama City, another ship would take them up the Pacific coast to California. During the first few years of the gold rush, there was a shortage of ships from Panama to San Francisco. This dearth of vessels meant that thousands of people were left waiting for a ship to take them north to California. Some came down with yellow fever and malaria, a disease transmitted by mosquitoes, and many travelers contracted cholera and died while waiting for ships to San Francisco.

The trip to California aboard a ship dubbed *Balance*, due to set set from New York City to Sacramento, California, in January 1849, cost each passenger $150, a hefty sum of money at the time. Included in that price were sleeping accommodations, meals, and "5 cubic feet [a

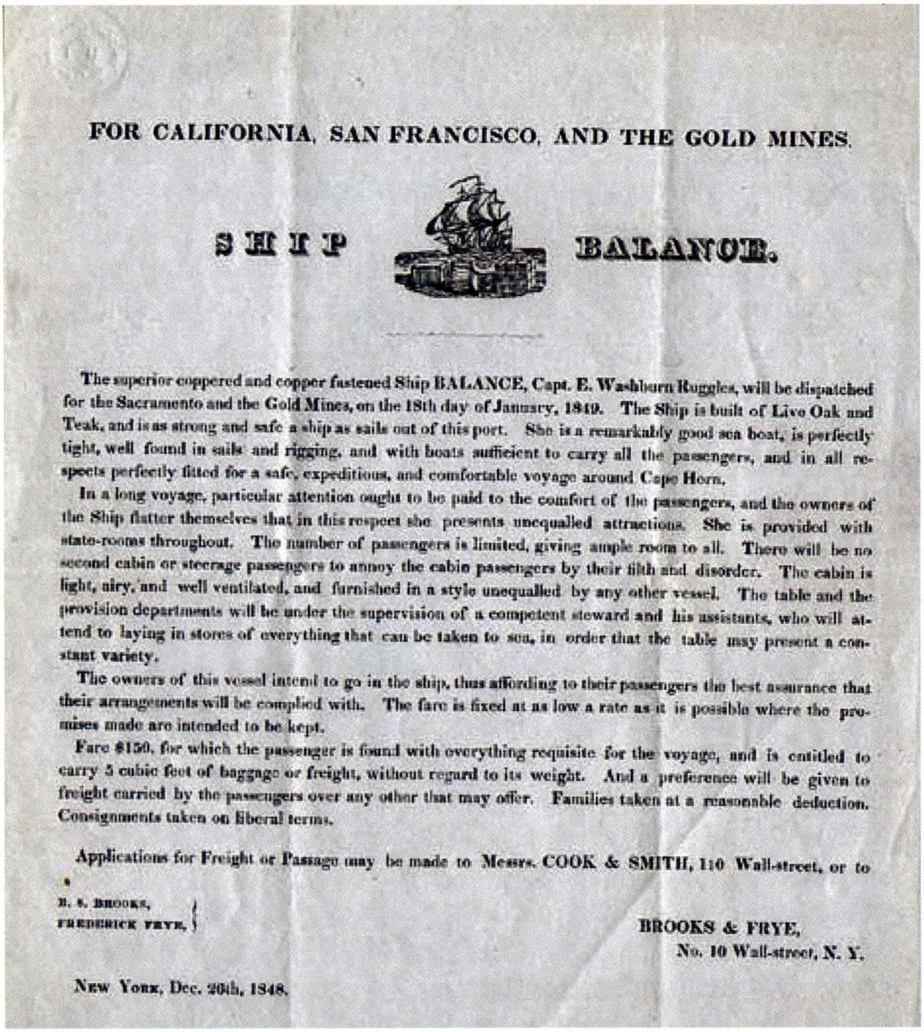

FOR CALIFORNIA, SAN FRANCISCO, AND THE GOLD MINES.

SHIP BALANCE.

The superior coppered and copper fastened Ship BALANCE, Capt. E. Washburn Ruggles, will be dispatched for the Sacramento and the Gold Mines, on the 18th day of January, 1849. The Ship is built of Live Oak and Teak, and is as strong and safe a ship as sails out of this port. She is a remarkably good sea boat, is perfectly tight, well found in sails and rigging, and with boats sufficient to carry all the passengers, and in all respects perfectly fitted for a safe, expeditious, and comfortable voyage around Cape Horn.

In a long voyage, particular attention ought to be paid to the comfort of the passengers, and the owners of the Ship flatter themselves that in this respect she presents unequalled attractions. She is provided with state-rooms throughout. The number of passengers is limited, giving ample room to all. There will be no second cabin or steerage passengers to annoy the cabin passengers by their filth and disorder. The cabin is light, airy, and well ventilated, and furnished in a style unequalled by any other vessel. The table and the provision departments will be under the supervision of a competent steward and his assistants, who will attend to laying in stores of everything that can be taken to sea, in order that the table may present a constant variety.

The owners of this vessel intend to go in the ship, thus affording to their passengers the best assurance that their arrangements will be complied with. The fare is fixed at as low a rate as it is possible where the promises made are intended to be kept.

Fare $150, for which the passenger is found with everything requisite for the voyage, and is entitled to carry 5 cubic feet of baggage or freight, without regard to its weight. And a preference will be given to freight carried by the passengers over any other that may offer. Families taken at a reasonable deduction. Consignments taken on liberal terms.

Applications for Freight or Passage may be made to Messrs. COOK & SMITH, 110 Wall-street, or to

H. S. BROOKS,
FREDERICK FRYE,

BROOKS & FRYE,
No. 10 Wall-street, N. Y.

NEW YORK, Dec. 26th, 1848.

This advertisement, which was likely posted around New York City on December 26, 1848, alerted the public of the sail date of the ship *Balance*, bound from New York City to Sacramento, California. (For a transcription, see pages 53–54.)

three-dimensional measurement of a foot] of baggage or freight, without regard to its weight." Brooks and Frye also make sure to mention the following fact, "There will be no second cabin or steerage passengers to annoy the cabin passengers with their filth and disorder." ("Steerage" referred to a section of a ship with inferior accommodations that was occupied by passengers who paid the lowest fare.) This statement was likely made to attract an upper-class group of passengers who could pay a higher price for their passage. It was likely that they were glad to pay the high rate for a guarantee that they wouldn't have to share tight living quarters with lower-class passengers who had purchased steerage tickets.

GOLD OR GOD?

As demand for transportation to the goldfields increased, so did the price. Soon, a ticket could cost between $500 and $1,000. To gold seekers, this seemed a small price to pay compared to the riches that lay waiting in California. In the months between April 1849 and January 1850 alone, as many as forty thousand people may have reached San Francisco by sea to find their fortune. However, not everyone was in search of gold and material wealth. A few passengers among the throngs of gold seekers had more idealistic reasons for making the trip west.

A daguerreotype of Reverend Joseph A. Benton. He is shown seated in formal dress, perhaps the same clothing he wore when preaching to his congregation aboard the *Edward Everett*.

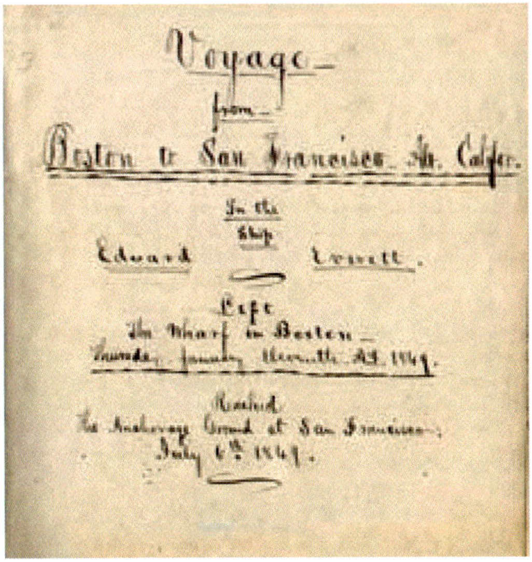
Voyage
from
Boston to San Francisco
In the
Ship
Edward Everett.
Left
the Wharf in Boston
Reached
the Anchorage Ground at San Francisco,
July 6th 1849.

After Reverend Benton reached Sacramento in July 1849, he established the First Church of Christ, also called the Pioneer Congregational Church. As noted in his diary, seen here, days after arriving Benton delivered his first sermon from his wagon to about 100 men and three women gathered in the grove of trees.

One such passenger was Reverend Joseph A. Benton, a Protestant clergyman who went to California to preach the word of God to the people there. Reverend Benton set sail from Boston aboard the *Edward Everett*, accompanying members of the Boston and California Joint Stock Mining and Trading Company.

During the long voyage, Reverend Benton not only preached sermons to the passengers, he also held discussions on religious topics. He kept a diary aboard the ship and after he reached California, describing the experience in detail. Here we see the title page from Benton's diary.

Upon the *Edward Everett*'s arrival in San Francisco, the sight that greeted Reverend Benton and the other passengers was likely much like the scene shown on page 31. In the months and years after Marshall discovered gold at Sutter's Mill, San Francisco became the prime destination for gold seekers from around the globe. Before Marshall's discovery, San Francisco had been a quiet little port with a population of

This view of San Francisco, California, by William Birch McMurtrie (1816–1872) represents San Francisco Bay as seen from atop Telegraph Hill in April 1850. Among the subjects depicted are wharves, abandoned ships, and the prospectors' tents and rickety wooden shacks.

perhaps one thousand people. Just a few years later, it had quickly grown into a boisterous city of nearly thirty thousand people, most of them Argonauts.

San Francisco didn't go through the many years of growth and development that most cities experienced. It became an instant city of canvas tents and hastily built wooden structures that provided only the most basic shelter for the anxious prospectors who arrived at San Francisco Bay.

★ CHAPTER FOUR

WESTWARD HO!

One thing should be made clear at this point. Gold was not the only thing that brought Americans to California. Years before Marshall ever spied those two nuggets of gold, people from the East had been making their way west, mapping out routes across the continent toward California as well as Oregon. These pioneers, who came to be known as overlanders, crossed the grassy prairies of the plains, the treacherous passes of the Rocky Mountains, and the arid deserts, all the while transporting their possessions in wagons that often broke down or were lost in flooded rivers.

It was a very difficult and often dangerous journey. Sickness and disease claimed many lives, and severe weather often took many more—or, at the very least, delayed travel and made living conditions miserable.

THE OREGON TRAIL

The Oregon Trail made its way through about 2,000 miles (3,220 km) of plains, deserts, and mountains, beginning at Independence, Missouri, and ending in

This letter sheet, "Hutchings' Panoramic Scenes—Crossing the Plains," features "views drawn from nature in 1853" by famous gold rush–era artist George Holbrook Baker, who drew thirteen separate scenes depicting the experiences of overlanders heading west along the Oregon Trail.

the Pacific Northwest. In the years following Marshall's discovery at Sutter's Mill, many groups of overlanders gathered near the Missouri River at Independence,

OVERLANDERS

The overland routes that the pioneers had established became more crowded with migrating gold seekers. Many prospectors who didn't like the idea of a journey by sea took to the overland trails. The gold-seeking overlanders followed the lead of those who had made the journey by boat, often forming large joint-stock companies for the trip west. Technically, joint-stock companies are groups of people who come together to run a business, drawing from a joint stock of capital owned by individual members of the company. However, in the case of the overlanders, these companies banded together for a common purpose, sharing their resources in order to help one another reach California's goldfields.

Some joint-stock companies were arranged informally and often consisted of family members or groups of friends and neighbors. In larger eastern cities, such as Boston, Philadelphia, and New York, companies sometimes formed when people responded to newspaper advertisements for overland treks to California. Once the companies were formed, the overlanders had to choose which transcontinental path they would take to ensure the quickest and least difficult journey. Many relied chiefly on the longest of the overland trails that the pioneers had blazed in the decade leading up to the gold rush–the Oregon Trail.

Missouri, to start out on their journey west. Before the trip even began, many things had to be considered. Often, people had to camp on the Missouri River's eastern bank, waiting for spring vegetation to grow to avoid the risk of starving their animals. If they waited too long, however, they could be caught in the mountains when severe winter weather struck. This delay could mean freezing to death or starving if the animals died from the harsh elements or lack of food. Timing was crucial, and new difficulties would face them as they set out across the plains.

On a day without unexpected delays or difficulties, the wagon trains could cover about 10 to 15 miles (15–25 km). On a bad day, they might not even move an inch. Once on the trail, the travelers were on their own. Dangers had to be faced as a group, or all would fail. Any hardship—whether hunger, sickness, injury, severe weather, buffalo stampedes, or broken equipment—had to be overcome using whatever resources were available within the group, or with the help of a company that was close by on the trail. With only their fellow travelers to help them, the overlanders had to be prepared for anything.

BUYING TOOLS; GETTING SCHOOLED

The transcontinental travelers also made sure they were prepared to dig for gold and haul it away once they found it. They wanted to be sure they had every tool they would need in their quest for fortune. Many shopkeepers and merchants in towns along the westbound trails took advantage of the prospectors' enthusiasm, convincing them that they simply had to have certain items in order to strike it rich in California. While they did sell some necessary goods—oxen, mules, guns and

This lithograph by Henry R. Robinson was published around 1850. The image, brimming with satire, shows a man traveling to California in search of gold, overladen with many useless items.

gunpowder, and pack-saddles—they also promoted worthless things such as "automatic gold washers" and "goldometers." Some merchants told the overlanders that they could trade these items with the Native Americans along the trail for gold.

This lithograph pokes fun at the overlanders. The following dialogue appears on the top of some versions of the lithograph: "I am sorry I did not follow the advice of Granny and go around the Horn, through the Straights, or by Chagres," says the overlander. Rather than choosing the sea route and traveling around Cape Horn or via Chagres [Panama], this cartoon overlander represents all those inexperienced—or "greenhorn"—travelers who loaded themselves down with every imaginable appliance, items that usually had to be dumped along the trail later to lighten their loads.

CHAPTER FIVE

THE LIFE OF A MINER

The life of the average miner can be summed up in one word: difficult. The first mining camps—clusters of canvas tents set up around the miners' claims—sprang up immediately after Marshall's discovery at Sutter's Mill. A claim was a tract of land that had been staked out by a miner as his own. Rising with the sun, a miner would eat a sparse breakfast of biscuits and coffee, and then spend the day digging for gold with a pick and shovel.

PANNING

Panning was a slow, painstaking process: put dirt in a pan, add water, and swish the mixture around. Little by little, the dirt would wash over the pan's edge. If there was gold in the dirt, the gold would remain in the pan because it was heavier. Even if the miners found gold, they usually didn't find more than a few dollars' worth a day. As time passed, miners began to build new tools to help them sift through greater amounts of soil than they could by panning. They

In this engraving, miners are cradling for gold, a process in which gold is separated from dirt. Cradling was less efficient than panning, but it allowed miners to process more dirt and usually resulted in more gold found at day's end.

invented the "rocker" or "cradle," an open trough set atop a base that could be rocked back and forth to "wash" larger amounts of dirt. Any gold would stick to wooden strips at the bottom of the cradle.

When dusk fell, the miners would return to their tents for dinner—usually pickled meat and coffee. When the sun went down, there was little to do but go to bed or play poker and drink whiskey by the fire.

POP-UP TOWNS... AND SHOPS

Soon, many of the small mining camps grew into busy towns. In particularly gold-rich districts, hundreds and sometimes thousands of Argonauts would settle in these towns. Eager merchants settled there as well, ready to make their own fortune by supplying miners with items they needed, such as food, clothing, and tools. They also set up saloons and gambling halls to provide entertainment to the weary miners. The lifestyle took its toll on many who succumbed to weaknesseses for liquor and gambling.

Although reality usually proved them wrong, some miners believed that if they worked very hard and avoided the temptations of the mining towns, they would be rewarded for their clean living.

This 1849 photograph shows a group of miners at a gold mine in Taylorsville, California.

CODES AND COMMANDMENTS

The life of a miner was a favorite topic for satire during the gold rush. There were definite codes of conduct miners were supposed to follow, regardless of whether they had a virtuous or "sinful" lifestyle. The letter sheet seen on page 41, *The Miner's Ten Commandments*, combined text and illustrations to poke fun at mining life and the "miner's code."

The first commandment was short and simple: "Thou shalt have no other claim than one." This was an actual rule found in many mining codes throughout the area at the time—a miner was allowed to work only one gold claim at a time. The eighth commandment was often considered the most difficult: "Thou shalt not steal a pick, or a shovel, or a pan, from thy fellow miner, nor take away his tools without his leave . . . for he will be sure to discover what thou hast done, and will straightway call his fellow miners together, and if the law hinder them not, they will hang thee, or give thee fifty lashes, or shave thy head and brand thee, like a horse thief, with R upon thy cheek, to be known and read of all men, Californians in particular."

In other words, a miner was forbidden to steal a pick, shovel, or pan from another miner—or borrow his tools without permission—because the other miner would find out and immediately call the other miners together. If the law didn't intrude, they would either hang the offending miner, whip him fifty times, or shave his head and burn the letter R onto his cheek (much like a horse thief), so that everyone else—especially people in California—would know of his crime. Though the letter sheet was satirical, such statements reflected actual punishments for crimes that were committed among the miners.

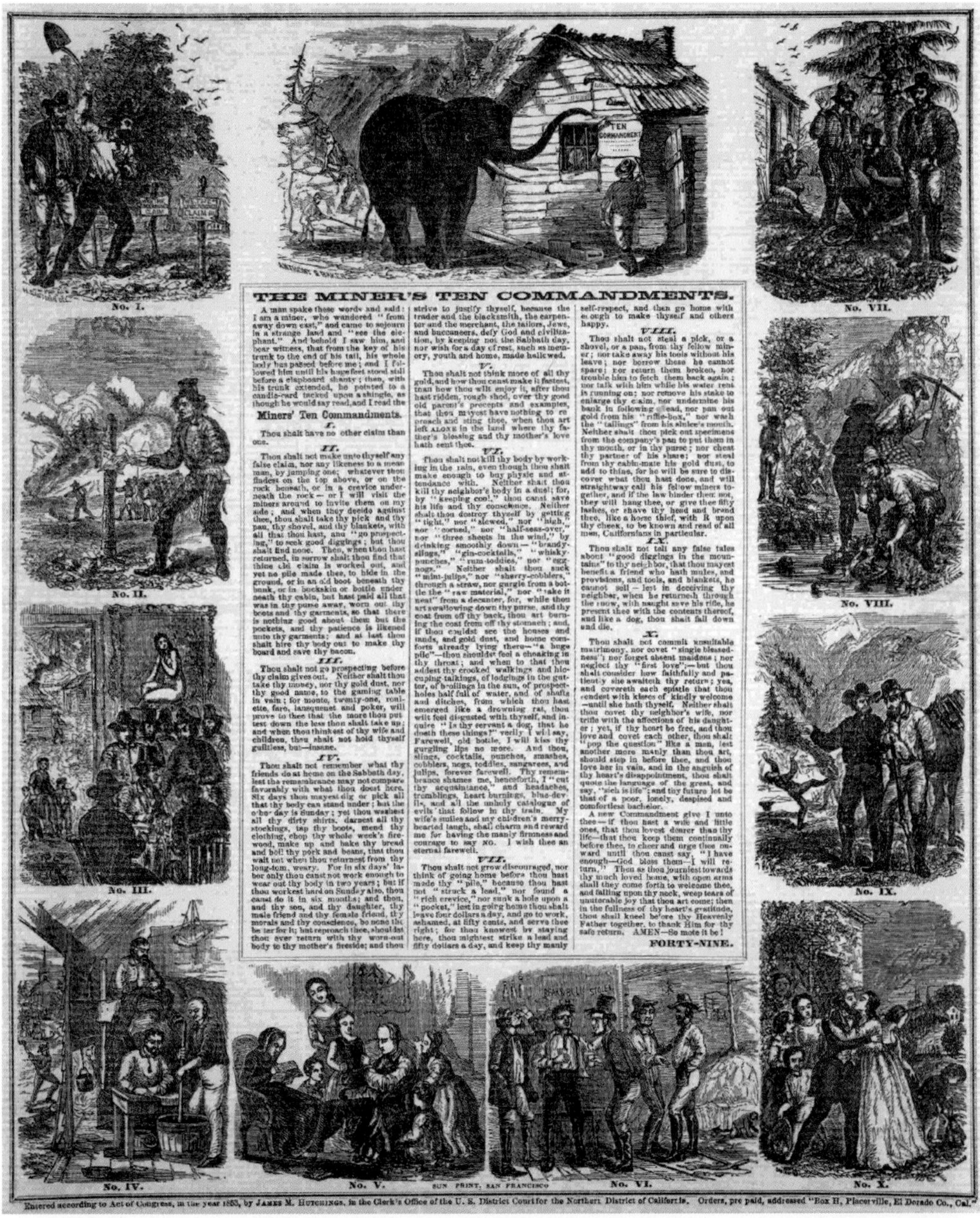

THE MINER'S TEN COMMANDMENTS.

A man spake these words and said: I am a miner, who wandered "from away down east," and came to sojourn in a strange land and "see the elephant." And behold I saw him, and bear witness, that from the key of his trunk to the end of his tail, his whole body has passed before me; and I followed him until his huge feet stood still before a clapboard shanty; then, with his trunk extended, he pointed to a candle-card tacked upon a shingle, as though he would say read, and I read the

Miners' Ten Commandments.

I.

Thou shalt have no other claim than one.

II.

Thou shalt not make unto thyself any false claim, nor any likeness to a mean man, by jumping one: whatever thou findest on the top above, or on the rock beneath, or in a crevice underneath the rock — or I will visit the miners around to invite them on my side; and when they decide against thee, thou shalt take thy pick and thy pan, thy shovel, and thy blankets, with all that thou hast, and "go prospecting," to seek good diggings; but thou shalt find none. Then, when thou hast returned, in sorrow shalt thou find that thine old claim is worked out, and yet no pile made thee, to hide in the ground, or in an old boot beneath thy bunk, or in buckskin or bottle underneath thy cabin, but hast paid all that was in thy purse away, worn out thy boots and thy garments, so that there is nothing good about them but the pockets, and thy patience is likened unto thy garments; and at last thou shalt hire thy body out to make thy board and save thy bacon.

III.

Thou shalt not go prospecting before thy claim gives out. Neither shalt thou take thy money, nor thy gold dust, nor thy good name, to the gaming table in vain; for monte, twenty-one, roulette, faro, lansquenet and poker, will prove to thee that the more thou puttest down the less thou shalt take up; and when thou thinkest of thy wife and children, thou shalt not hold thyself guiltless, but—insane.

IV.

Thou shalt not remember what thy friends do at home on the Sabbath day, lest the remembrance may not compare favorably with what thou doest here. Six days thou mayest dig or pick all that thy body can stand under; but the other day is Sunday; yet thou washest all thy dirty shirts, darnest all thy stockings, tap thy boots, mend thy clothing, chop thy whole week's firewood, make up and bake thy bread and boil thy pork and beans, that thou wait not when thou returnest from thy long-tom, weary. For in six days' labor only thou canst not work enough to wear out thy body in two years; but if thou workest hard on Sunday also, thou canst do it in six months; and thou, and thy son, and thy daughter, thy male friend and thy female friend, thy morals and thy conscience, be none the better for it; but reproach thee, shouldst thou ever return with thy worn-out body to thy mother's fireside; and thou strive to justify thyself, because the trader and the blacksmith, the carpenter and the merchant, the tailors, Jews, and buccaneers, defy God and civilization, by keeping not the Sabbath day, nor wish for a day of rest, such as memory, youth and home, made hallowed.

V.

Thou shalt not think more of all thy gold, and how thou canst make it fastest, than how thou wilt enjoy it, after thou hast ridden, rough shod, over thy good old parent's precepts and examples, that thou mayest have nothing to reproach and sting thee, when thou art left ALONE in the land where thy father's blessing and thy mother's love hath sent thee.

VI.

Thou shalt not kill thy body by working in the rain, even though thou shalt make enough to buy physic and attendance with. Neither shalt thou kill thy neighbor's body in a duel; for, by "keeping cool," thou canst save his life and thy conscience. Neither shalt thou destroy thyself by getting "tight," nor "slewed," nor "high," nor "corned," nor "half-seas-over," nor "three sheets in the wind," by drinking smoothly down — "brandy-slings," "gin-cocktails," "whisky-punches," "rum-toddies," nor "egg-nogs." Neither shalt thou suck "mint-juleps," nor "sherry-cobblers," through a straw, nor gurgle from a bottle the "raw material," nor "take it neat" from a decanter, for, while thou art swallowing down thy purse, and thy coat from off thy back, thou art burning the coat from off thy stomach; and, if thou couldst see the houses and lands, and gold dust, and home comforts already lying there—"a huge pile"—thou shouldst feel a choaking in thy throat; and when to that thou addest thy crooked walkings and hiccuping talkings, of lodgings in the gutter, of broilings in the sun, of prospect-holes half full of water, and of shafts and ditches, from which thou hast emerged like a drowning rat, thou wilt feel disgusted with thyself, and inquire "Is thy servant a dog, that he doeth these things?" verily I will say, Farewell, old bottle, I will kiss thy gurgling lips no more. And thou, slings, cocktails, punches, smashes, cobblers, nogs, toddies, sangarees, and julips, forever farewell. Thy remembrance shames me, henceforth, I "cut thy acquaintance," and headaches, tremblings, heart burnings, blue-devils, and all the unholy catalogue of evils that follow in thy train. My wife's smiles and my children's merry-hearted laugh, shall charm and reward me for having the manly firmness and courage to say NO. I wish thee an eternal farewell.

VII.

Thou shalt not grow discouraged, nor think of going home before thou hast made thy "pile," because thou hast not "struck a lead," nor found a "rich crevice," nor sunk a hole upon a "pocket," lest in going home thou shalt leave four dollars a day, and go to work, ashamed, at fifty cents, and serve thee right; for thou knowest by staying here, thou mightest strike a lead and fifty dollars a day, and keep thy manly self-respect, and then go home with enough to make thyself and others happy.

VIII.

Thou shalt not steal a pick, or a shovel, or a pan, from thy fellow miner; nor take away his tools without his leave; nor borrow those he cannot spare; nor return them broken, nor trouble him to fetch them back again; nor talk with him while his water rent is running on; nor remove his stake to enlarge thy claim, nor undermine his bank in following a lead, nor pan out gold from his "riffle-box," nor wash the "tailings" from his sluice's mouth. Neither shalt thou pick out specimens from the company's pan to put them in thy mouth, or in thy purse; nor cheat thy partner of his share; nor steal from thy cabin-mate his gold dust, to add to thine, for he will be sure to discover what thou hast done, and will straightway call his fellow miners together, and if the law hinder them not, they will hang thee, or give thee fifty lashes, or shave thy head and brand thee, like a horse thief, with R upon thy cheek, to be known and read of all men, Californians in particular.

IX.

Thou shalt not tell any false tales about "good diggings in the mountains" to thy neighbor, that thou mayest benefit a friend who hath mules, and provisions, and tools, and blankets, he cannot sell — lest in deceiving thy neighbor, when he returneth through the snow, with naught save his rifle, he present thee with the contents thereof, and like a dog, thou shalt fall down and die.

X.

Thou shalt not commit unsuitable matrimony, nor covet "single blessedness"; nor forget absent maidens; nor neglect thy "first love";—but thou shalt consider how faithfully and patiently she awaiteth thy return; yea, and covereth each epistle that thou sendest with kisses of kindly welcome —until she hath thyself. Neither shalt thou covet thy neighbor's wife, nor trifle with the affections of his daughter; yet, if thy heart be free, and thou love and covet each other, thou shalt "pop the question" like a man, lest another more manly than thou art, should step in before thee, and thou love her in vain, and in the anguish of thy heart's disappointment, thou shalt quote the language of the great, and say, "sich is life"; and thy future lot be that of a poor, lonely, despised and comfortless bachelor.

A new Commandment give I unto thee — if thou hast a wife and little ones, that thou lovest dearer than thy life—that thou keep them continually before thee, to cheer and urge thee onward until thou canst say, "I have enough—God bless them—I will return." Then as thou journiest towards thy much loved home, with open arms shall they come forth to welcome thee, and falling upon thy neck, weep tears of unutterable joy that thou art come; then in the fullness of thy heart's gratitude, thou shall kneel before thy Heavenly Father together, to thank Him for thy safe return. AMEN—So mote it be!

FORTY-NINE.

Entered according to Act of Congress, in the year 1853, by JAMES M. HUTCHINGS, in the Clerk's Office of the U. S. District Court for the Northern District of California. Orders, pre paid, addressed "Box H, Placerville, El Dorado Co., Cal."

The Miner's Ten Commandments by author and editor James M. Hutchings, published in 1853, is the best-known example of a satirical look at a miner's life. Miners found it entertaining, many using it to decorate their tents or shacks. More than 100,000 copies were sold in just one year.

The miners soon learned that the tales of gold nuggets the size of a man's fist were exaggerated, and many days, weeks, or months might pass before a miner found any gold at all. In the meantime, the miner would have to find another way to make a living. Men from the East who had been well respected and held well-paying jobs now found themselves doing whatever job they could find in exchange for lodging and food.

The life of riches the emigrants had envisioned rarely matched their real lives. Those prospectors who did manage to accumulate some wealth would often send money back home to their families. By doing so, they could earn their families pride and lessen the feelings of loneliness that sometimes seemed overwhelming. Companies began to spring up that allowed Argonauts to transfer money safely from California to points throughout the country. Modern banking was beginning to take shape.

★ CHAPTER SIX

CALIFORNIA SCHEMING

Although the promise of better lives brought thousands to California, the reality of bad behavior—letting greed and not higher principles guide their thoughts and deeds—became reality for many of the Argonauts. Some set aside their principles and acted in ways they would have never dreamed of before. The promise of instant wealth also attracted unscrupulous bandits who traveled around the region stealing what they liked from those who either couldn't defend themselves or found themselves outnumbered.

This hand-colored woodcut depicts vigilante "hounds" in San Francisco sometime in the 1850s, attacking Chileans and other Catholic immigrants. Finding gold held no assurance of keeping it.

The threat of violence was a constant presence in and around the mining

THE PLACE WE HEAR ABOUT

The grimness of life in California was a strong theme in much of the artwork and social commentary of the period. In this lithograph, entitled *The Place We Hear About*, violence breaks out as miners and thieves fight over gold.

In the background of *The Place We Hear About*, the Capitol, in Washington, D.C, and the White

It is believed that an artist named S. Lee Perkins drew this lithograph in around 1849. In it, a man in the center fires a gun at a miner who is carrying a large gold-filled sack. Men around them battle with fists and knives. Illustrating the difficult living conditions and near starvation some experienced in the goldfields, one man demands another to give him food, exclaiming: "Bread! Bread! Damn you! Bread."

House can be seen, as well as President James K. Polk and members of his cabinet, who carry pick-axes and shovels as they travel down the "High Road to California." Polk exclaims, "Off Boys to reap the reward of our four years labour." This was likely a direct jab at the political situation in the United States during the period. The United States had taken the territory of California from Mexico in February 1848 after winning the war it had been fighting with Mexico for nearly two years. This happened during Polk's presidency, and many viewed the president as a gold-hungry man more interested in gold than in the country's welfare. Perkins, the artist, seems to agree.

camps, evident in the hand-colored woodcut seen on page 43. Its message is clearly based in the reality of the times. If a miner found gold, he might also find a knife at his throat.

THE LAWLESS WEST

Most of California's mining towns didn't have formal laws—just the "miner's code," rules that listed a miner's rights and responsibilities as a member of the mining community. There were no police to uphold the laws and no real jails to hold offenders. When laws were violated, other miners took justice into their own hands, often handing out harsh punishments. If a person were caught stealing, he might be branded so that people would know his crime, or he might be publicly flogged. If a man were accused of murder, he didn't get a lawyer to defend him or have his case heard in front of a judge and jury.

If a citizens' committee found him guilty, he could be publicly hanged. As a result, innocent men were sometimes killed for crimes they didn't commit, and the guilty often went free.

By 1850, California had enough people to be admitted to the United States as the thirty-first state. As the population grew, so did the crime rate—but without the luxury of time to develop a strong justice system to deal with offenders. Frustrated with the situation, a group of merchants came together in 1851 to form a Committee of Vigilance, taking matters out of the hands of elected government officials. The committee, which had about 700 members, set about preventing immigrants from disembarking at the city's docks, deporting people for crimes, and hanging accused murderers. The committee was dissolved within two months, only to reform in 1856.

THIS LAND IS OUR LAND (AND THAT INCLUDES THE GOLD)

S. Lee Perkins was also fiercely patriotic when it came to the United States' right to California's gold, as seen in another lithograph he is thought to have done entitled *The Defence of the California Bank*. In this political cartoon, the artist expresses the widely held opinion that California's treasures belonged to Americans and had to be kept safe from the greedy hands of foreign powers.

GOLD, BUT AT WHAT COST?

American distrust of foreign interests wasn't limited to leaders of other countries—it carried over to immigrant miners as well. California had become home to large numbers of Chinese, Australian, Mexican, and Latin American immigrants,

Published in 1849, *The Defence of the California Bank* was probably drawn by S. Lee Perkins. Leaders from around the world—depicted as odd human/animal mash-ups—are clearly after California's gold.

to name just a few ethnic groups that came to California in search of gold and a better life. Americans from the East who had gone west for gold and settled in California were often racist and blamed California's problems on immigrants whose traditions and cultures they didn't understand. Bigotry was a strong force, and many innocent foreign immigrants wrongly accused of crimes they didn't commit were lynched during the gold rush simply because their skin wasn't white. In 1850, a law was passed requiring foreign miners to pay twenty dollars a month for a mining permit. This caused much conflict between American and immigrant miners, and it was repealed the following year. California's state legislature tried again in 1852, setting the foreign miner's tax at three dollars a month. This, coupled with the hostile discrimination and violence they faced each day, was enough to make many foreigners return to their home countries. Those who stayed often left the mining communities and cities so they might live in peace, finding work on rural farms instead. Native Americans and Californios (people of Mexican descent who had lived in California since it was a Mexican territory) watched sadly as California was corrupted by the eastern prospectors' greed.

Soon the frenzied call of riches beyond one's wildest dreams that had beckoned hopeful Argonauts from all over the world to the rolling hills of California began to lose its luster. Some people's dreams had been realized and they had emerged with their golden prize, but most people's dreams had faded away, replaced with the realities of rough living and meager results. Within just a few years of James Marshall's discovery of gold at Sutter's Mill, fewer and fewer people came to California, and those who did were far outnumbered by those who left. By the mid-1850s, many mining camps looked like ghost towns. Although the gold rush had happened just a few years before, people now told stories about what life had been like back then, when the lure of gold was all that mattered. To many, it had quickly become a distant memory.

In the end, though, California's gold rush left an indelible mark upon the land, changing the face of the United States. It opened up the West and led to the first transcontinental railroad linking the East to California. New cities such as San Francisco and Sacramento sprang up and grew quickly, and western territories—such as California—were admitted into the Union. Perhaps most important, many different people from many different cultures had become inextricably woven into the fabric of America.

TIMELINE

1839 John Sutter arrives in California and convinces Mexican governor Juan Bautista Alvarado to give him a land grant for 50,000 acres (20,234 ha).

July 1845 James Wilson Marshall arrives at Sutter's Fort after traveling on a wagon train from Oregon.

May 13, 1846 The Mexican War begins between Mexico and the United States.

July 1846 Although the Mexican War still rages, the U.S. flag is raised on Yerba Buena Island in San Francisco Bay.

August 1847 John Sutter hires James Marshall to build a sawmill in Coloma, California. Marshall and his men begin work on Sutter's Mill the following month.

January 24, 1848 Marshall finds gold in a stream near Sutter's Mill.

February 2, 1848 The Mexican War ends with the signing of the Treaty of Guadalupe Hidalgo. California is now an official U.S. territory.

March 15, 1848 The first story about Marshall's discovery of gold appears in a San Francisco newspaper. It is largely ignored.

May 1848 The first wave of gold miners arrives at Sutter's Fort.

July 1848 Colonel Richard B. Mason, military governor of California, tours Coloma and confirms that there is gold there.

December 5, 1848 President James K. Polk delivers the news of California's gold to Congress, displaying a box of gold dust as evidence.

February 1849 The first shipload of miners arrives in San Francisco Bay aboard the vessel *California*.

May 1849 The first overland wagon trains begin their transcontinental journey west to California.

April 1850 The Foreign Miners' Tax is put into place, charging foreign miners (particularly those of Mexican or Chinese descent) twenty dollars a month to mine in California.

September 9, 1850 The territory of California officially becomes the thirty-first state in the Union.

March 14, 1851 The Foreign Miners' Tax is repealed.

June 9, 1851 The San Francisco Committee of Vigilance is formed.

September 1851 The San Francisco Committee of Vigilance is dissolved.

1852 Gold becomes hard to find in California. Many miners return to their homes, both in the United States and other countries. Women and children begin to arrive in large numbers to join their husbands and fathers who have settled in California.

PAGE 14: TRANSCRIPTION OF LEASE AGREEMENT

Gesn, Colule and Lole their heirs and assigns they paying the said Sutter and Marshall a reasonable price for the mill and buildings that may be put on the said premises by them.

In Witness whereof the said parties of the second [cross out] first and second part set their names and seals, done this the fourth day of February in the year of our Lord one thousand eight hundred and fourty eight.

Witnesses	Pulpuli	x	his chief mark	Seal
Charles Bennet,	Gesn	x	his chief mark	Seal
William Scott.	Colule	x	his alcalde mark	Seal
	Lole	x	his alcalde mark	Seal
	J. A. Sutter,			Seal
	James W. Marshall.			Seal

Done in the presence and with my aprobation
J. A. Sutter—
???? Indian Agent—

CONTEMPORARY ENGLISH TRANSLATION:

Gesn, Colule, and Lole and their heirs will pay Sutter and Marshall a reasonable price for the mill and buildings they may build on the land.

To show that they agree to this, Pulpuli, Gesn, Colule, Lole, Sutter, and Marshall have signed this and put their seals on it. This was done February 4, 1848.

This was done in my presence and with my approval.

PAGE 19: TRANSCRIPTION OF "CARRIERS' ADDRESS"

1.

Come on good friends—all other things giver o'er,
We'll talk of Gold, on California's shore,
Gold! the great end and aim of human strife;
The all-exciting stimulus of life.
O, Power Supreme! man's earliest offerings shine
As votive gifts around thy glittering shrine.
Forever kneeling at thy altars proud,
Behold a suppliant, fawning, cringing crowd,
There offering up peace, honor, virtue, health,
To gain an entrance to the heaven of wealth.
Time was—time is—when gold's almighty sway
The high and low—the small and great obey.
It changes ill to good, and wrong to right;
Makes the *disgusting* fill us with delight.
The mean and groveling are, presto! made
Noble and generous, by its potent aid.
Tinged with its glare, the basest crimes assume
To mortal eyes the hue of virtue's bloom;
Changes the prate of fools to sayings good—
Makes dulness wit, *not*
always understood!

2.

A beast that has it, with the gods is ranged,
A man without it to a beast is changed.
So by the almighty influence of gold
Fashion and morals both are thus controlled.
A line is drawn between the rich and poor,
Which no presumptuous mortal must pass o'er.
Give me but gold, you give me virtue, wisdom, grace,
Raise me at once to fashion's highest place;
And saints and sinners bow down and adore—
Not me in truth, but my rich glittering ore.
No wonder then the world is going mad—
No wonder then that thousand hearts are glad
To hear of regions in the far-off West,
With all untold, unthought-of treasures blest;

Where mother earth her golden treasures yields
Not to such toil as tills New England fields,
But places free before her outstretched hand
Her stores exhaustless of the glittering sand.

3.
Go then, ye slaves, to California's shore
Go delve and dig, and grasp the precious ore.
Leave home and friends, and all the heart holds dear,
There seek a comfort for each sorrow here,
Find all it needs, to make you rich and great,
To live in more than Dives' royal state,
To every want and every wish supply,
And then, poor delvers, give it up—and die!
While greedy heirs, expectant for your death,
With greedy eyes, shall watch your passing breath,
With outward woe, but inward joy profound,
Behold you safely nestled in the ground.
Well, you may die—your heirs possess your gains—
But still exhaustless from those distant plains,
With ceaseless flow, on rolls a golden tide
Till the most craving wishes are supplied;
Till, Midas-like, gold only meets our sight,
And sun and moon shine with a golden light.

PAGE 28: TRANSCRIPTION OF *FOR CALIFORNIA SAN FRANCISCO, AND THE GOLD MINES*

For California, San Francisco, and the Gold Mines. Ship Balance.

The superior coppered and copper fastened Ship BALANCE, Capt. E. Washburn Ruggles, will be dispatched for the Sacramento and the Gold Mines, on the 18th day of January, 1849. The Ship is build of Live Oak and Teak, and is as strong and safe a ship as sails out of this port. She is a remarkably good sea boat, is perfectly tight, well found in sails and rigging, and with boats sufficient to carry all the passengers, and in all respects perfectly fitted for a safe, expeditious, and comfortable voyage around Cape Horn.

In a long voyage, particular attention ought to be paid to the comfort of the passengers, and the owners of the Ship flatter themselves that in this respect she presents unequalled attractions. She is provided with state-rooms throughout. The number of passengers is limited, giving ample room to all. There will be no second cabin or steerage passengers to annoy the cabin passengers by their filth and disorder. The cabin is light, airy, and well ventilated, and furnished in a style unequalled by any other vessel. The table and the provisions departments will be under the supervision of a competent steward and his assistants, who will attend to laying in stores of everything than can be taken to sea, in order that the table may present a constant variety.

The owners of this vessel intend to go in the ship, thus affording to their passengers the best assurance that their arrangements will be complied with. The fare is fixed at as low a rate as it is possible where the promises made are intended to be kept.

Fare $150, for which the passenger is found with everything requisite for the voyage, and is entitled to carry 5 cubic feet of baggage or freight, without regard to its weight. And a preference will be given to freight carried by the passengers over any other that may offer. Families taken at a reasonable deduction. Consignments taken on liberal terms.

Applications for Freight or Passage may be made to Messrs. COOK & SMITH, 110 Wall-street, or to

B. S. BROOKS
FREDERICK FRYE,
BROOKS & FRYE,
No. 10 Wall-street, N. Y.

New York, Dec. 26th, 1848.

GLOSSARY

amenity A feature that is considered pleasant or agreeable.

Argonaut A name for gold rush–era miners in search of gold.

brand To mark by burning the skin with a hot iron.

cholera A disease usually characterized by severe distress in the stomach and intestines.

delirium A mental disturbance characterized by confusion, hallucinations, and disordered speech.

dysentery A disease usually caused by infection that is characterized by severe diarrhea.

editorial A newspaper or magazine article that expresses the opinions of the publication's editors or publishers.

emigrant A person who leaves the place where he or she lives to live somewhere else.

emigrate To leave the place where you live to live somewhere else.

engraving A picture made from a metal plate that has an image carved into it.

forty-niner A person who went to California in search of gold in 1849.

gristmill A mill for grinding grain.

immigrant A person who leaves the country where he or she lives to live in another country.

isthmus A narrow strip of land that connects two larger pieces of land.

lease A contract by which one person or party passes land or real estate to another person or party, usually for a specified time period for a specified rent.

lithograph A print that is made by printing from a plane surface, such as a metal plate, on which the image to be printed is ink receptive and the blank area is ink repellent.

malaria A disease caused by parasites in the red blood cells, usually transmitted by the bite of a mosquito, that is often characterized by frequent attacks of fever and chills.

migration A movement from one place or country to another.

morality A system of virtues and rules of conduct.

prospector A person who explores an area, usually for mineral deposits like gold.

repeal To do away with something, as a law, by legally revoking it.

satire A literary device by which human vices, sin, and foolishness are pointed out and ridiculed.

telegraph A communication system in which coded signals are sent over an electric wire.

trough A long, shallow container.

vigilance committee A volunteer committee of citizens that comes together to punish criminals when the processes of law are incapable of doing so.

wagon train A line of wagons usually carrying supplies for a group of settlers who are traveling overland.

yellow fever A disease caused by a virus transmitted by the bite of a mosquito. Yellow fever is characterized by physical exhaustion, fever, protein in the urine indicating kidney disease, a yellowish cast to the skin, and often internal bleeding.

FOR MORE INFORMATION

California Historical Society
678 Mission Street
San Francisco, CA 94105
(415) 357-1848
Website: http://www.calhist.org
The California Historical Society features exhibitions and programs that show how the state's history impacts its residents' contemporary lives. One of its collections is about the gold rush and includes journals, guides, and daguerreotypes of miners.

California Museum
1020 O Street
Sacramento, CA 95814
(916) 653-7524
Website: http://www.californiamuseum.org
The California Museum celebrates the history of California and the contribution of its residents to arts and culture.

California State Mining and Mineral Museum
Mariposa County Fairgrounds
Mariposa, CA 95338
(209) 742-7625
Website: http://www.parks.ca.gov/?page_id=588
The California State Mining and Mineral Museum hosts a collection of more than thirteen thousand objects, including mining artifacts and mineral specimens. Visitors can tour the mine tunnel and observe a model of a stamp mill to visualize how gold was extracted from rock in the mid-1800s.

Empire Mine State Historic Park
10791 East Empire Street
Grass Valley, CA 95945

(530) 273-8522
Website: http://www.empiremine.org
At Empire Mine State Historic Park, visitors can tour a mineyard and blacksmith shop to learn about mining in the area, which took place from 1850 until 1956. Visitors can also go hiking or geocaching.

Geological Society of America
3300 Penrose Place
Boulder, CO 80301-9140
(303) 357-1000
Website: http://www.geosociety.org
The GSA is a professional organization of earth scientists, including those who work in universities, government, business, and industry. Its headquarters has several exhibits featuring diverse rock specimens.

Klondike Gold Rush—Seattle Unit National Historic Park
319 Second Avenue South
Seattle, WA 98104
(206) 220-4240
Website: http://www.nps.gov/klse/index.htm
This national historic park focuses on the 1897 Klondike gold rush to the Yukon in remote northwestern Canada and particularly the role of Seattle as a way station for people traveling there.

WEBSITES

Because of the changing nature of Internet links, Rosen Publishing has developed an online list of websites related to the subject of this book. This site is updated regularly. Please use this link to access the list:

http://www.rosenlinks.com/UAH/Gold

FOR FURTHER READING

Ansary, Mir Tamim. *California History* (State Studies). Portsmouth, NH: Heinemann, 2009.

Benoit, Peter. *The California Gold Rush* (Cornerstones of Freedom). New York, NY: Scholastic Children's Press, 2012.

Brown, Don. *Gold! Gold from the American River!* New York, NY: Roaring Brook Press, 2011.

Collins, Terry. *Into the West: Causes and Effects of U.S. Westward Expansion* (Cause and Effect). North Mankato, MN: Capstone Press, 2013.

Duffield, Katy S. *California History for Kids: Missions, Miners, and Moviemakers in the Golden State.* Chicago, IL: Chicago Review Press, 2012.

Holub, Joan. *What Was the Gold Rush?* New York, NY: Grosset & Dunlap, 2013.

Landau, Elaine. *The Gold Rush in California: Would You Catch Gold Fever?* (What Would You Do?) Berkeley Heights, NJ: Enslow Elementary, 2015.

Levy, Janey. *Life During the Gold Rush* (What You Didn't Know About History). New York, NY: Gareth Stevens Publishing, 2013.

Musolf, Nell. *The Split History of Westward Expansion in the United States* (Perspectives Flip Books). North Mankato, MN: Compass Point Books, 2012.

Otfinoski, Steven. *A Primary Source History of Westward Expansion.* North Mankato, MN: Capstone Press, 2015.

Roza, Greg. *Westward Expansion* (The Story of America). New York, NY: Gareth Stevens Publishing, 2011.

Walker, Paul Robert. *Gold Rush and Riches* (All About America). London, England: Kingfisher, 2011.

BIBLIOGRAPHY

Altman, Linda Jacobs. *The California Gold Rush in American History.* Berkeley Heights, NJ: Enslow Publishers, Inc., 1997.

Blodgett, Peter J. *Land of Golden Dreams: California in the Gold Rush Decade, 1848–1858.* San Marino, CA: Huntington Library Press, 1999.

ComSpark. "Gold Rush Chronicles." 1998. Retrieved January 30, 2015 (http://www.comspark.com/chronicles).

Kurutz, Gary F. "California as We Saw It: Exploring the California Gold Rush." California State Library. 2000. Retrieved January 30, 2015 (http://www.library.ca.gov/goldrush).

Library of Congress. "California as I Saw It." 1998. Retrieved January 30, 2015 (http://memory.loc.gov/ammem/cbhtml/cbhome.html).

Oakland Museum of California. "California's Untold Stories: Gold Rush!" 1998. Retrieved January 30, 2015 (http://www.museumca.org/goldrush).

Sacramento Bee. "Gold Rush." Retrieved January 30, 2015 (http://www.calgoldrush.com).

Schanzer, Rosalyn. *Gold Fever! Tales from the California Gold Rush.* Washington, DC: National Geographic Society, 1999.

Van Steenwyk, Elizabeth. *The California Gold Rush: West with the Forty-Niners.* Danbury, CT: Franklin Watts, Inc., 1991.

Virtual Museum of the City of San Francisco. "San Francisco Gold Rush." Retrieved January 30, 2015 (http://www.sfmuseum.org/hist1/index0.1.html#gold).

INDEX

L

M

N

O

P

S

ABOUT THE AUTHORS

Longtime writer and editor Melanie Gildenstein lives in San Francisco, California, where she pans for stories.

Kerri O'Donnell received her degree in journalism from New York University. She is a writer and editor currently residing in Buffalo, New York.

PHOTO CREDITS

Cover Print Collector/Hulton Archive/Getty Images; p. 3 Lone Wolf Photography/Shutterstock.com; pp. 4–5 (background) Enigmangels/Shutterstock.com; p. 5 (inset) © Ivy Close Images/Alamy; pp. 7, 15, 23, 32, 37, 43 (background) optimarc/Shutterstock.com; pp. 8, 11, 13, 14, 18, 19, 20, 24, 25, 28, 29, 30, 31, 33, 36 California State Library; p. 38 Time Life Pictures/The Life Picture Collection/Getty Images; p. 39 Huntington Library/SuperStock; p. 43 (inset) © North Wind Picture Archives; pp. 41, 44, 47 Library of Congress Prints and Photographs Division; cover, p. 1 design elements Piotr Krzeslak/Shutterstock.com (flag), Aleksandrs Bondars/Shutterstock.com (scroll); cover and interior pages background textures chudo-yudo/Shutterstock.com, Alina G/Shutterstock.com, Attitude/Shutterstock.com, sl_photo/Shutterstock.com

Designer: Michael Moy; Executive Editor: Hope Lourie Killcoyne